POOR PERSON'S PROSE POETRY

By

Scott Wagner

To Two very special People

Love Scott, LEANNE, MORGAN and FAYE xxxx

Each poem is protected by copyright, no copying or distribution permitted; either in part, or in whole.

Published by Wagner's Poetry Publishers

CONTENTS   PAGE

2

3

READ THIS FIRST PLEASE

I would like to thank you for your courage to take a look
At this, an unknown poet's very own book
The point of this book is to purely entertain
I do not wish to cause you the reader any anguish or
pain

Each poem that I have written, at least all rhyme
I very much hope that you will enjoy, each and every
line
Just enjoy each poem as a bit of harmless rambling
The sentiment of some mean a lot, but some don't
mean a thing
So if you're offended by anything that I have written
then I really do apologise
But I have never claimed to be ALL knowing and wise

I know it's customary for writers to thank their family
for all their support
But this has been a solo effort; my wife's help has fallen
way short
Never mind, not being loved or cared for is a frequent
occurrence for me
But at least I have fond memories of writing all this
poetry!

Happy Reading....

OFFICE BULLY

An oaf from work says that he is going to give me a
smacking
Because when he ran for union rep, he didn't get my
backing
If he's dumb enough to tell me when he's going to give
me this kicking
I'll arrange the day before for me to go missing

I know he likes anything that's all blood, guts and gory
But I'll try my best to dissuade him with a nice little
story
"Listen up mate, picture if you will a hot sunny day
You're crossing the road when this beautiful woman
starts walking your way
You can do nothing but stand still and stare
Taking in her beauty, especially her long blonde hair
That nice fitting sun dress caressing her every curve
You want to go and talk to her but you haven't got the
nerve
She gives you a little smile and then begins to pose
Letting you know without doubt, you're the one she
chose"

He's now looking into space and he's even beginning to
drool
I can't believe he's listening to this, he really is a fool
I continued, "She turns towards you slightly showing off
her chest

I bet that's a place that your face would like to rest
Then you hear music playing softly, just like a dozen angels humming
It distracts you just long enough, so that you don't see that bus coming!"

DRIVING WITH KIDS IN THE BACK

Driving down the motorway in my MPV
My wife, my son, my daughter and me
It's a spacious family car which drives really well
But from all the moaning coming from the backseat, you
wouldn't be able to tell

I never got driven round in such luxury and style
When I was younger, going any distance in a car was
really quite a trial
Vibration, road noise and a crackly radio was all that I
got
Smooth ride, sunroof, CD player, my kids have got the
lot

If I asked "Are we there yet?" any more than twice, my
dad would make it very clear
That if I said it one more time, I would get a clip round
the ear
You can't make that threat any more though much to
my sorrow
Because the kids know as well as me, that that threat is
completely hollow

So I put up with the phrase "Are we there yet?" and
"This is so boring!"
But my wife gave them a fright once by saying, "Dad
can't hear you over his snoring!"

After their screams had died down when they realised it
wasn't true
It backfired on me badly, as they both then said they
needed the loo!

FITNESS CHEAT

A friend of my wife told her something that I didn't
think was wise
And that was the fact that I was lazy and needed some
exercise
So she bought me some trainers and a running vest
Then added that a five mile jog would be an adequate
test

The most I've ever run was about five metres before
And that's only when it's been raining, and then only
from my car to the front door
To impress her though I set off at an incredible pace
Nothing like a jog, much more like an all out race

I ran far enough around the corner so that she couldn't
see
I then stopped and thought to myself, that's enough
running for me
So I strolled round the streets for an hour or so
Faking tiredness as I returned home, I really put on a
convincing show

She told me well done; now you can sit down and take a
rest
She then said "I hope you pass every other fitness test?"

Each night she sent me out and I'd just nip down to the pub
Where I'd drink a swift pint and scoff down some grub

I got fed up though and told myself, that enough's enough
I'm giving up this charade and if she doesn't like it, then it's just tough
She sent me out again, but after ten minutes I turned round and returned home
Where I found her in bed with my best mate Jerome!

HANGMAN'S HELL

Sitting all alone in the hangman's cell
There was a large crowd outside waiting to bid me
farewell
I've eaten my last meal, when the jailer comes to tell me
it's time
I now have to pay the price for my hideous crime

He jangled the keys in the lock as he opened the door to
get me out
He showed me that he hated me; I was left in no doubt
As I was led outside the gathered crowd all booed and
jeered
They then threw rotten veg, it was worse than I had
feared

Everyone there despised me and they definitely wanted
me dead
The hangman told me he was adding weight to my legs,
so the rope would rip off my head
I paused at the base of the ladder which led to the
gallows above
The impatient jailer pleased the crowd, by giving me a
shove

The time has come said the voice from inside me
Do I walk to my death, or do I try and flee?

But I was harassed all the way up the ladder, right up to the top
Where the hangman gladly showed me, how far I was going to drop

I handed the hangman a letter that I had already wrote
And in exchange he put the noose, very roughly round my throat
Battered and bruised by all the veg that was thrown
The crowd were baying for blood, there was no mercy shown

I stood on the gallows when calm descended all over me
When all of a sudden, there was only one face in the crowd that I could see
I know I'm someone who's infamous and will be remembered for all time
But I don't know who I am, or what on earth was my crime?

I woke up with a jolt as I fell through the trap door
I then felt an incredible urge, to put both of my feet on the floor.

I HATE MY JOB

I'm totally fed up with my job and my boss
But I'm not skilled enough to leave, and he's not
someone you cross
He barked at me, "I've tried phoning, e-mailing, but
you're a hard man to contact"
I need to tell you about changes I've made to your
contract

I want you to work a little bit more everyday
Oh and there's no extra money in it, for you by the way
It makes me mad as they penny pinch everywhere
But the real working conditions, they just don't seem to
care

I'm tired of being pushed about by health and safety
rules
What's wrong with these people, do they think we're all
fools
They add a little bit to my work each and every day
And not once in this democratic process, do I get a say

I'm sick of looking out of my window, out over the
parking lot
Being forced to look at the cars that everyone has got
My boss and directors all have fancy luxury cars
I get relief at night though, when I can at least look at
the stars

The cars at least are easy on the eye it has to be said
Then I glance over to my transport, locked up in the bike shed
At least I know one way or another, each working day will end
It's the only thought that's stops me from going round the bend.

NIGHTCLUB WOES

I wanted to get a girlfriend so I decided to go out
clubbing
But it was just an overcrowded cattle market, with lots
of pushing and shoving
In-spite of the fact that all the women were putting on a
show
Whenever I talked to them, they all seemed to be
programmed to say "No"

I spent all night getting nowhere, but spending an awful
lot of money
And have some guy spill beer on me, which he found
really funny
I decided that I was far too classy for this disgusting
joint
My tuxedo and cravat I felt reinforced the point

So I went to the wine bar, which I always go to when I'm
feeling blue
No admission fee or ticket required, the doormen just
waved me through
There at the bar I saw this really beautiful filly
She beckoned me over but I got shy and said, "Oh, don't
be silly"

What was I doing, it was clear that she at least liked me
Should I call her lady or act hip and trendy, and go and
call her "Baby?"
When I sat down next to her on this really low bar stool
The view that gave me, was enough to make me drool

My evening's exploits so far weren't good it had to be
said
So I immediately apologised for missing the signals, I
think that I've just read
"Sorry miss, I didn't mean to offend you, please don't
call the police?"
Just my luck, when all the confusion was over, it turned
out she was my long lost niece!

BIKE CRASH

Driving my car to the shops just the other day
I was in a really bad mood, so God helps anyone who
gets in my way
Then from absolutely nowhere, I got this brilliant idea
An idea for a sonnet, about a pint of beer

I must write it down before I forget
I know if I don't I'm sure to worry and fret
But the shops were shutting in a few minutes time
Against the law I know, but I thought it would be fine

I groped around the glove box for a pen and paper
I found an old boiled sweet and an ice scraper
Then on the floor of the car I spotted a paper and a pen
So I temporarily took my eyes, off the road again

Grabbed them both, then got my eyes back on the road
Just as I was closing in on a lorry with a sign saying,
"Extra Wide Load"
I slowed up in time and then thanked my lucky stars
That if I hadn't stopped in time, I could've ended up
behind bars

Careless driving nowadays gets you locked up by the law
My friend got jailed for accidentally hitting, a parked car
opened door

But this was too good to stop, so I began writing my wonderful sonnet
When all of a sudden this cyclist went flying over my bonnet!

ALONE

Lying there on the couch just watching some TV
When my wife came in from the kitchen, and she said to
me
"We need some milk and a loaf of bread
I'll nip to the shop," were the words she said
Blowing me a kiss and then shutting the door
I'm thinking I'm a lucky man that's for sure

About an hour went by and she hadn't come back
It was cold and wet outside, and she had no anorak
When there was a knock at the door, and I thought
she's forgotten her key
I opened the door and to my surprise, there was a
policeman looking at me
He said, "I've got some bad news please may I come
in?"
"Of course" I replied, with a nervous grin

"There's been an accident and your wife has sadly died"
My first thought was, why had this policeman lied?
"Walking along the pavement with a pint of milk and
some bread
A man lost control of his car, because of the wet roads
he said
But I could smell his breath which reeked of beer
And I wasn't even standing, all that near"

My broken world in tatters, this nightmare has just
begun
I then asked the policeman, "What will I tell my two
year old son?
Who's sleeping soundly upstairs in his bed
Dreaming of the fairytale that his mummy had read"

I couldn't explain to my son why mummy's no longer
here
I kept breaking down, but I knew I must persevere
The day of the funeral had soon came around
The day that I would lay my young wife into the ground
I was holding up quite well 'til our son waved her
goodbye
At that moment I couldn't do anything, but breakdown
and cry

He still keeps asking when mummy's coming home
I tell him as gently as I can, that were now on our own
Because how can you tell your two year old son
That some selfish drunk man used his car as a gun

As we stand by her graveside and lay down some fresh
flowers
We'd be there for a few minutes, but for him it seems
like hours
I pray at the grave "Please look out for us love
From your vantage point, high up above"
He wonders why I stare and cry at a grey lump of stone

As he doesn't yet know, this is his mummy's eternal home.

CHRISTMAS

It's Christmas Eve and Santa's in the sky
Being pulled by his reindeer, way up high
To bring you presents if you've been really good
In the olden days you know, all the toys were made of
wood

I expect you wonder how he can fit down the chimney
I wandered that myself, so I asked, and he told me
"I have in my possession a special magic key
That opens any lock, but only for me"

"A chimney is not needed for me to get in
And I certainly don't need ever to be thin
I put the key into the lock and say a special rhyme
And the door then opens for me, time after time"

"I guess you may ponder how I do it all in one night
The task looks impossible but I manage it alright
The key to the answer is in the list I have read
The names of good boys and girls are all stored in my
head"

"You see I do not have to go to every house in one night
Because I don't go to houses where the children bicker
and fight
This narrows the amount of homes I go to you see

So I can go to all the good children, and leave presents by the tree"

"I get a hand written letter from your mum and dad
It tells me how well behaved you've been, and all the times you were bad
I then balance this up against all the times you were good
Do you deserve to go on my list; well tell me do you think you should?
The only way you'll know is on Christmas day
I hope that you have been good, as the next festive season is a long time away."

I FINALLY GOT MY WAY

It took several weeks for me to get my way
But I've convinced my wife to have a U.K. holiday
I now only have the U.K. weather God to appease
My strategy will be simple; I'll get on my knees and beg,
"Pretty please"

It doesn't have to be hot, as long as it doesn't rain
Or else in my neck or my bum, my wife will be a
constant pain
I chose somewhere where's there's bound to be some
sun
So that my wife and I can enjoy ourselves, and have a
little bit of fun

The place that I chose was glorious historic Cornwall
The week that I picked though, turned out to have the
heaviest rainfall
With the look on my wife's face I could tell that she
wasn't impressed
So we made our way home early, both of us thoroughly
depressed

She said "Next year my holiday will be abroad in the sun
And just so you understand, it will be a holiday just for
one!

HOW MUCH?!!!!!!!!!!!!!

The wall needed rendering on the side of my house
According to my "Always right" loving spouse
So I called on my builder friend, whose name is Syd
And he quoted me a staggering nine hundred quid
My voice going quite high I said, "Nine hundred
pound?"
He answered, "Do you want some help mate, picking
your jaw off the ground?"

How can a few bags of cement and a big bag of sand
Cost me the fee of nearly a grand
Hundred pounds for supplies, the rest is for time, tax
and toil
But he's an old friend of mine, so I feel I must be loyal
He justified the cost by saying my bricks are all shot
But that's not my fault; they're the only ones I've got

He set to work erecting each piece of scaffold
They reminded me of Syd as they're all rusty and old
My job in this deal was to make him lots of tea
Nothing more was needed, and that suited me
I'll give him his due he worked hard every day
And I think in the end he'd earned his money I'd say

The job now done and he's come to get paid
I joked "The cupboard is bare there's no money I'm
afraid"
He looked at me with a disappointed look in his eye

"I'm only joking" I said, "There's no need to cry"
I gave him his money and I took back my mug
"I'd wash that properly" he said "As I think I've picked up a bug"

Were still good friends and he visits me often
But that joke I played on him has not been forgotten
I'm a Paver by trade and I paved his garden
He then pulled the same joke on me and I sternly replied, "I beg your Pardon?"
"The cupboard is bare there's no money I'm afraid"
Not being as compassionate as Syd, I hit him with my spade!

I'M NOT A COWARD

I can't believe you called me a yellow belly
Just because I don't act like a hero you see off the telly
Calling me gutless, wimpy and weak
And laugh at my broken voice every time that I speak

So I'm breaking up with you and I'm calling it a day
How's that for assertiveness from me by the way
So when you get this message on your answer phone
Don't call me back, because I won't be at home

You never ever really loved me that much I know
You would let go of my hand when we met anyone we
know
And yet I saved your life once by distracting that bee
My screams and arm waving, made that bee follow me
But you didn't think to thank me or even give me a
cuddle
Just because while running away, I pushed you in a
puddle

I can't believe you said I did nothing when you were
mugged
As he strolled away, I made sure you were well hugged
And with no thought to my own safety as he could have
had a knife
I stood there and gave him the frowning of his life

Your pet never liked me, and I had to fight each time to get near you
I would struggle to overpower her; I admit that much is true
And after the fight, my clothes would be left all dirty and scruffy
But you would always take her side, that damn cat fluffy

You can keep all the things I bought you, including that cuddly teddy
I don't want reminders of you around, because I'm just not ready
Well have a nice life, but don't call me when you get this message
Because I know all you'll do is start shouting, and become very aggressive.

PUB FIGHT FRIGHT

I accidentally knocked this guy's arm in the pub
He very childishly went to my table, and then spat in my grub
I said sorry and offered to buy him a drink
He replied "Reckon that makes everything alright then do ya, I don't think"

He then in a very aggressive way shouted, "Now you, Come here!"
I'm a poet not a fighter, so I stood there trembling with fear
Stepping back a bit he retreated his arm getting ready to punch me on the nose
Doing this he inadvertently elbowed a really BIG guy, and also stood on his toes

He went from hero to zero in the blink of an eye
As he begged for forgiveness from this really BIG guy
But the big guy was having absolutely none of it
Handing his drink to his mate he quipped, "Hold it, while I knock him about a bit"

The one who was going to hit me squealed like a girl while filling his pants, just like a baby
A pleasant afternoon had gone horribly wrong; the situation's just gone crazy
A black eye or two later he'd learned his lesson I think

But my mates and I didn't hang around for long,
because of the awful stink!

LABOUR PAINS

I never really wanted any kids in my life
But that all changed when my girlfriend became my wife
Getting her pregnant was a great deal of fun
She wanted a girl, but I prayed for a son

The day came and she was wheeled into delivery
She then got all moody, whiny, and a bit of a misery
She screamed and panted and made a bit of a mess
Blood on the floor and sweat on her pillow, not
appealing I must confess

After hours of her moaning a baby boy had arrived
But much more importantly, my intensely squeezed
hand had survived
I was told I was insensitive when I got out the measuring
tape
And then gave my wife a month, to get herself back in
shape

I was now inconsiderate as well, as I sat there drinking
my tea
She said "You've made yourself one, but what about
me?"
"I didn't just get mine; I also got one for the midwife
Because you took your time, she's wasted several hours
of her life"

Gazing at my newborn son, I realised he looked just like me
At least when he's older he'll attract the women easily!

ME AND MY MOTORBIKE

Years ago when I had my own motorbike
I was happy, carefree, and could go where I like
I rode a 500cc and it rode like a dream
Our styles complimented each other, like a well drilled
team

Shaft driven, it motored me across the ground
Purring like a big cat, what a beautiful sound
I used to wear skateboard pads strapped to each knee
To try and stop arthritis infecting me

I would go out in any kind of weather
Strapped to my handlebar for good fortune, was my
lucky heather
I always rode with my lights on full
As I steamed through the standing traffic like a raging
bull

If any cars pulled to the side to let me by
I'd thank them by raising my left hand to the sky
The best time to ride is in the summer
In Britain that's only a few days though, it's a bit of a
bummer

I'd spend a lot of time polishing her up
If I'd enter her in a beauty contest, I'm sure she'd win a
cup

First place I must add, she's that beautiful to me
It wasn't cheap though, it cost me a lot of money

I had to sell her though and it really broke my heart
But whenever anyone viewed her, she would never ever
start
My new girlfriend couldn't understand why this was the
case
But unfortunately for me, she learnt to read my face

Her old man knew a bit about the internal combustion
engine
He noticed the spark plugs missing from my gleaming v-
twin
This didn't go down too well with my girlfriend you see
So she made me choose there and then, "The damn
motorbike or me?"

YET ANOTHER LITTLE RANT

I would like to tell you something that makes a lot of
sense
And for once I'm not going to just sit there, perching on
the fence
Why do we pay road tax, and then pay tax again on fuel
I don't know about you but it makes me feel a fool

To add insult to injury, there are now charges on certain
parts of the motorway
As well as endless double yellows, and the ever growing
pay and display
Congestion charging is the newest way to get extra
money out of us
But as usual we all lie down and take it and don't make
a fuss

We pay council tax that goes up without fail each and
every year
And get given more and more rules by them, to which
we must adhere
We recycle our own rubbish into bins and then leave
them by the kerb
If I said this about ten years ago then it would be
laughed off, as being quite absurd

Each weekday morning we got our post twice a day
Now it arrives just once, and it could be any time of day
It's the twenty first century and life shouldn't be this way
Well now I've had my rant, I can once again pack my soapbox away.

MY LITTLE VAN

I used to own a little van to take me to and from work
But my girlfriend would never get in it, just in case some
people would smirk
It's only a small van but I could cram a lot in
That's when my circle of friends really started growin'

I used to lend my van to one of my friends
He told me on the straight it went well, but not so good
on the bends
He would borrow my van a bit more than just once or
twice
He offered me money, but I wouldn't take it, not at any
price

It took us all over the place despite the fact it's all rusty
and battered
And the seat springs twanged and the engine clattered
But it never let me down in all the time that I owned it
Although it was starting to look really tatty, that much I
will admit

Just before its M.O.T was due, I decided to trade it in
The salesman took my van for a car, with a handshake
and a grin
When I told my friend about what I'd done he smacked
me on my knee

And added "You're NOT the only one who uses it you know, you didn't consult me!"

MY LITTLE BOY'S WETSUIT

I bought my little boy a neoprene wet suit
For practical reasons, as well as the fact that it looked cute
It would keep his skin safe from all of the sun's harmful rays
And he could still play in the paddling pool, on the cooler days

But my boy didn't share my enthusiasm though
He was fine at first, but after a while it began to show
He was moaning and complaining while putting it on
This was now a struggle and all the fun had now gone

Through his tears he kept saying "No dad, I don't want to"
My caring sharing parenting replied, "Son, of course you do!"
But he wriggled and squirmed as I squeezed him into his suit
He was crying and whining, when in came his mum and called me a brute

I know he would love it if he just gave it a try
I don't understand his objections, there's no need to cry
I'll admit it was a bit of tight fit and I forgot to remove the tag

By now though, even my interest in his new present was
beginning to flag

I got the suit on him and zipped it right up to his chin
Still crying and whimpering I said "Fine, I give in,
What is it you don't like about this present from me?"
He replied "I love the suit dad, I just need a wee!"

OUR FIRST HOME

Our first home we bought together was virtually a shell
It would have been most people's idea of a living hell
With no hot water or even gas central heating
Our new young trendy lifestyle, was taking a bit of a
beating

With no insurance we gambled and lit the coal fire
The smoke that came into the room, was as if we'd lit a
car tyre
Next thing we knew we had our neighbours banging on
our door
"Smoke's filling up our living room" they cried, I said
"Are you sure?"

As if someone is going to lie about something like that
"You must switch the fire off, it's choking our cat!"
Putting the fire out I got all mucky and dirty
I turned on the tap to wash my hands and I cried, "Oh
blinking bertie!"

This was my family's traditional expression, whenever
we got a surprise
We're boring really, we never ever swear, shout or tell
lies
The water coming out of the tap was really very hot but
neither of us knew why

My girlfriend was just so happy; you could see a tear in
each eye

We later found out it was the back boiler behind the
coal fire
Great, but we can't use the fire, a chimney sweep was
what we needed to hire
The chimney swept I bought a smoke bomb, then told
next door what I'm going to do
I lit the bomb, went next door to see smoke coming out
through their fire from their flue

So for two and half years we lived with no heat
But boring we may be, but we're not easily beat
The valley of depression we were always able to bridge
Because whenever we wanted any heat in the winter,
we simply opened the fridge!

THE DUMB POSTMAN

The dumbest person I ever met, has to be my post-man
He delivered every day in his little red van
One day he left a parcel in my shed with a note
"Parcel in shed" were the simple words he wrote

Some time had passed when I got a call from Marcel
From the person who had sent me that little blue parcel
Wanting to know if I liked it or not
I told him this was a parcel that I never got

I reassured him that I would ask the post-man
And we both agreed that that was the best plan
Asking the post-man whose name was Fred
He said, "Yes, I left it in your shed"

"Well why didn't you leave a note" I exclaimed
He looked quite nervous; as I'm sure I'm not the first
who'd complained
He said "Come with me and I'll show you
I remember it well because the wrapping was blue"

He opened my shed and there it sat
He smugly stated "Well then, what's that?"
I picked the parcel up, and I then smiled at Fred
As on the package was the note, "Parcel in shed"

THREE THINGS YOU LOVE

My girlfriend asked me, "Name three things you love?"
To see if we're compatible, like a hand in a glove
I said that's easy, a cold beer and my truck
I stopped and thought for a minute, hell I was stuck

She started to look uneasy and just a little bit hurt
So I bought some more time, by saying I really liked her skirt
I looked in her eyes, what she was wishing
Then it occurred to me, the third thing is fishing
She crossed her arms and slumped into her chair
I asked for another go, but she said she didn't care
"Listen, I'm a hard working man who likes a cold beer
I'm just not a great thinker I think that much is clear"

"Thanks a lot" she said, "You've gone and ruined our date"
I now know what I should have said, but it was just too late
The fourth thing I love in this life is you
More than ever before, believe me it's true
Just give me one more chance that's all I ask
I can make you feel special; I know I'm up to the task

Although I said you're fourth, that's not really true
The one on the list I love most, really is you
So change your wrinkled frown to a smile
Have another beer and hang here for a while

If I wasn't spending quality time with you
Then I don't know what else I would want to do
My truck, beer and fishing are nothing compared to you
Look my nose hasn't grown, so it really must be true.

JAIL

I was puffing on a joint, but I told the police that I didn't
inhale
The judge didn't believe me either and sent me straight
to jail
I washed with only water in prison as I felt such a dope
Because clumsy old me, went and dropped my bar of
soap

An overweight sweaty transvestite was my friendly cell
mate
Who kept going on about wanting to take me out on a
date
Some hired goons turned up and told me to meet their
boss
And they made me understand that if I didn't, it would
make him really cross

As they left, they let it slip that it was because their boss
was feeling frisky
And before I went I was to go and see "Booze Boy", and
bring along some whisky
I knocked on the door, knowing full well I was going to
be used as a whore
They let me in and demanded that I, "Take off my
clothes and leave them on the floor,
But before you do, pour each of us a drink"
One came close to me and muttered "Oh, you stink"

He added "Don't you ever wash with soap?"
"Since I've been here" I smartly replied, "Nope!"

Luckily for me I was always someone who had a plan
They may be bigger than me, but this time they've
picked on the wrong man
One remarked "This guy's gonna give me such a thrill"
With my back turned to them, I slipped into their drinks
a sleeping pill
I left them there naked, all piled on the floor fast asleep
I went and got my cell mate, who eagerly dived on top
of the heap!

TRUE LOVE

How do you know if you truly are in love?
At the top of the stairs, would you give your partner a
shove?
Or would you pull them away and hold them tight?
And when lying in bed, hug them all night?

If you're in love, then give them your most precious
possession
Then to see how they react, make up a confession
If your treasured item comes back broke
Or even worse is sent up in smoke

How would you respond to your true love then?
Would you ever look at them the same way again?
Is it true love if you're always in a jealous rage?
And you feel the need to keep her out of reach of
others, in a metaphorical cage

One could say that you then love them too much
If you can't stand the thought of anyone else looking, or
trying to touch
If you don't mind them being watched, or someone else
having a grope
Does this mean you don't care enough, and have given
up hope?

What if you row a lot, does this mean you shouldn't stay together?
Or one is a "Matter of fact" person, and the other always needs their lucky heather
The truth is, there isn't really an answer to any of the above
Except you really shouldn't be with them, if you were tempted to shove!

TRAFFIC COP TROUBLE

Driving down the motorway at a hundred miles an hour
My six point seatbelt, is letting me feel every bit of its
power
I'm in total control of this exceptional speed machine
No close calls yet, so my underwear's still clean

I'm sick of spending my time though, looking in my
mirrors for a blue light
It doesn't get any easier each time I see one though; I
still get quite a fright
It's two a.m. and there's no-one else on the road but me
As I go past a traffic cop, he could look the other way
I'm sure quite easily

But no, he has to come and bring me to a stop
Lecture me on the dangers of speed, before taking me
to the cop shop
He's right of course, excess speed really can kill
But the problem with it though, is that it gives me such
a thrill

Slow down I must and slow down I will, because there's
no thrill if indeed you kill
So if you drive as fast as I used to do
Then I hope like me you get caught, by the good old
boys in blue!

PEEPING TOM

Looking from my vantage point, I can see in through her
window
The leaves are rustling gently so I'm moving really slow
The view is better from over here, that's where I'll be
looking from
I'm afraid to say that I'm just a plain old peeping tom

I don't mean any harm or to cause any distress
I just want to see this sexy woman, without her wearing
her dress
She's perfect in my eyes and she's all that I desire
But watching her this way I know, I'm really playing with
fire

I'm just way too shy to talk to her like any normal guy
I've approached her in the street and smiled, but I then
just walked on by
I hate myself for watching her in the fashion that I do
But it's the only way I can feel close to her, my adorable
sexy Sue

A tiny little part of me wants her to catch me in the act
I know that sounds ridiculous, but it really is a fact
At least it would mean that she'd know the truth
It would save going to plan B, which is me climbing on
her roof

I hope her husband really breaks her heart
Then I would be able to comfort her, until she's ready
for a fresh start
I know so much about her already, like her favourite
colour is red
I now only want to know is, what she's like in bed!

WHAT'S WRONG WITH ME?

I think that I'm a really sexy guy
But women don't think so and I really don't know why?
I look great even though I don't comb my hair
And once a-week without fail, I change my underwear
When my hair reaches my shoulders I never fail
To tie it all up into a macho looking pigtail

Why don't women seem to fancy me?
Surely all the women in the world, can't be crazy?
But I do like my beer and I am kind of lazy
The morning after the night before, for me is always
kind of hazy

I drive my old faithful pickup truck
Even cruising around in this doesn't bring me any luck
Am I destined for a life all on my own?
I've never had a girlfriend and I'm now fully grown

I tried my luck at a singles bar
The women looked like men, so I didn't get far
I thought I'd pay for love with a woman of the night
But she turned me down; I'm thinking something's not
right

Well it's about time I radically changed my outlook
And go for a girl who's kind of plain, but who can really
cook

So I hit the keys to the internet
I found a plain old girl that works as a vet
I want to stay with her for the rest of my life
So I got down on one knee and asked her to be my wife.

FUZZY INTERCOM

I own a logistics company along with my wife
We make a little money for a nice cosy life
We have a top spec PC and even some staff
I must be a great boss; as we all have a good laugh
But the one thing I've never upgraded, and that's our
fuzzy intercom
It turned out to be my undoing, where it all went badly
wrong

I have a very talented hard working, good looking PA
Though not as pretty as my wife, I can honestly say
On our fuzzy intercom my wife simply misheard
It really upset her, but she didn't say a word

When the PA left the office I noticed my wife was gone
And me still not knowing that something was wrong
I just assumed she had just taken an early lunch
When in charged her brother snarling, "I hope you can
you take a punch?"
I panicked, because he's bigger than me and I bruise
easily

"I love her with all my heart, after all she is my wife
We make love all night long; I truly love my life
I love your sister, she has that special touch
With you being her brother, I realise I'm saying far too
much"

I had an ex-sailor who was feeling quite faint
Because my office reeked, of the smell of fresh paint
My wife's brother was messing with our fuzzy intercom
I can tell you right now he heard it all wrong
I asked the sailor if he would like a tot of rum
He thought he overheard me ask, could I touch his bum?

This time though he didn't hit me, because he knows that I bruise easily
It's time to fix this intercom, as this time I heard it all wrong
I overheard an employee ask my wife, if he could see her thong
What he actually asked was, if she would see if I was going to be long!

ME, MY BOY, A STRANGER AND TWO WOMEN

I was out with my family doing our weekly shop
I only wanted to get the bare essentials, but she wanted
to get the lot
She was throwing this that and the other into our
shopping trolley
But she then went and threw out things I'd put in, it
made me feel like a Wally

I enjoyed though watching other women, some of which
were beautiful
And I always tried my best, to get a sly little eyeful
When my little boy told me that he needed to go to the
loo
I asked him discreetly if he wanted a number one, or a
number two?

He told me that he just wanted a number one, which for
me was a big relief
Among other things it means our time in the toilet
should at least be brief
So I asked the shop assistant to tell me where the toilets
are
To my boy's relief she said that they weren't very far

Opening the door to the toilet, trying not to touch the
door plate
Because some peoples personal hygiene, quite simply
isn't great

Luckily we are the only ones in there so he didn't need
to wait
As the look on his face suggested that if he had to, it
could have been too late

Then a guy came in and stood next to me at the toilet
stall
He was a wiry kind of guy, who must have been at least
six foot tall
My boy and I washed our hands and were just about to
leave
So as not to touch the handle, I pulled my hand inside
my sleeve

Two women nearby nudged each other when they
heard what my boy had just said
It was really embarrassing; I wished I could put a bag
over my head
He blurted out, "That man in there has a bigger one
than you?"
But he was referring to my moustache, and his
statement was actually true!

MY DRUNKEN PAL

He comes home from the pub all battered and bruised,
after taking one or two beatings
But he says he can't be an alcoholic, because he doesn't
go to the meetings
"I drink little but often" he's always stated
But it's now been a few years since he last dated

Because word got about that he likes to have a drink
But he's drinking way too much; well at least that's
what I think
He tells me he can quit whenever he wants to
But he's deluding himself, and I think even he knows it's
not true

He gets surly and aggressive after one or two
So he gets into fights, not just one but a few
If I say something then I'm simply interfering
He knows I'm talking but he's just not hearing

Life's been unfair to him he will adamantly claim
But as far as I'm concerned, he has only got himself to
blame
There's no more that I can do for him
But without my nagging, his chances of survival are very
slim

He needs to pay rent for the gutter outside the pub
"The John and Jim"
Because that's where I look first, whenever I go looking
for him
I locked him in his room once to try and get him to go
cold turkey
But it didn't go well as he would shake, throw up, wet
himself, and get really shirty

So I let him out once with sick on his shirt and pee on his
trousers, as he went off for a beer
Not just one but quite a lot, the odd thing was that he
came home in good cheer
There's only one word that he's scared of in his
condition
And that one solitary word is, Prohibition!

MY LAZY WIFE

I can't believe you can really be that lazy
To be honest honey it's really driving me crazy
Get off your useless butt, and go and clean this house
And for goodness sake, catch that damn irritating
mouse

Even the mouse though is complaining of the mess
Me and the mouse are both losing our hair, all caused
by unnecessary stress
I'll even show you how to use the vacuum cleaner
My lazy little wife thinks that I couldn't be meaner

A duster isn't very heavy or the dishwasher very hard
Even the cooker seems to baffle her, as all my dinners
are charred
But she operates the remote control for the telly
Which I think is testament to her ever expanding belly

She's my wife and doesn't have a real job
Except it seems from watching TV and stuffing her gob
She wants me to get in a cleaner to do all of her chores
And every Sunday dinner, I have to entertain the in-laws

If I get a cleaner to do all of your chores
I'm also going to get for the bedroom, some nubile
blonde whores

She claimed that I was being unfair
But she's pushed me to the limit, so I really don't care!

RACING THE RAIN

Running as fast as we can back to the car
With shopping in each hand, our parked car can't be far
The clouds are now getting darker and it's just about to rain
I am quite close to the car now, but I feel I'm running in vein

The raindrops are getting ready to race from the clouds up above
There just waiting to be given that extra little shove
They're going to time it so that I think I'm going to make it
Letting everyone see that I'm spectacularly unfit

I can see my car now parked half way down this lane
Then would you believe it, I could feel the cold, cold rain
It started quite gently, but then it came down with real fury
It was as welcome as a rapist finding out that it's an all female jury

Why is it I can never remember which pocket my car keys are in?
It's raining so hard now, that the car roof is making an awful din
Putting all of the bags into my left hand I then delved deep into my pocket

Cursing criminals, because if it wasn't for them I
wouldn't have had to have locked it

My wife was now catching me up, but couldn't
understand why I'm still stood there
Of all the days for this to happen, it's simply just not fair
When I tell her what I've done, I know she'll scream and
shout
The keys are still in the ignition, "Sorry love, but we're
locked out!"

SNOT

My girlfriend and I decided to go for a little walk
So that we could have a good old fashioned heart to
heart talk
I pulled *that* face so she started to tease
As she knew in the next few seconds, that I was going to
sneeze

The problem is she's fed up with my constant roving eye
I didn't catch what she had said, because a sexy woman
had just walked by
The woman pulled a horrible face while looking at me
Turning to my girlfriend I declared, "She's up herself
isn't she?"

She looked back at me and smiled which I thought was
nice
I concluded that woman was so badly dressed, that she
must have been in vice
Then I saw my reflection in a shop window and I simply
just froze
As I saw a huge long stringer dangling from my nose

I couldn't believe my girlfriend never said a word
Disgusted with her I argued, "But I thought you were my
bird?"
My girlfriend went into a shop but I decided to wait
outside

So I could watch all the pretty women, and try to
redeem some pride

This woman was approaching, who has a great set of
pins
My girlfriend can't see me, so I looked, this way
everybody wins
I wanted to look all tough and rugged, so I kept my lips
shut to smile
And breathed in to look thin, as she's the prettiest thing
I've seen by a mile
I took a large intake of breath and tried to look all
loveable
Staring at me I thought she was looking at my sexy
stubble; but I had inadvertently blown a huge snot
bubble!

TELEVISION

I would like to know if it's the world or just me
But are we as a society watching far too much TV
I can't believe I plan my evening around the telly
And I've now noticed as a result, I'm getting a big fat belly

I have even planned the layout of my room around my television
It's about time I stopped this, and make a difficult decision
I can't carry on letting this thing rule my life
For heaven's sake I've got a couple of kids and a beautiful wife

But there is some kind of draw to this box in the front room
But anything factual all seem to be doom and gloom
The world is dying here and people are dying there
But it's just happening so often now, that I've started not to care

The worst news you can imagine isn't that shocking any more
Its sounds heartless and rash to say, but believe me I'm sure

But the paradox is quite astonishing I really have to say
Because if you don't keep up with "What's on," your
social life fades away

If you don't know what's on then you're left in no doubt
When you meet up with people, you'll have nothing to
talk about
The weather is okay for the first minute or two
But then you'll start to struggle, it's very sad but it's true

So I've decided to keep on watching my TV
But only to keep my social life sanity
I've tried to get people to read an intellectual book
But in response I always get this glazed uninterested
look.

NUDIST BEACH

There was now only one more hurdle we needed to
breach
An old wooden style was the only thing between us, and
a nudist beach
A quick look round to see if anyone was watching us
My friend telling me to get on with it, and to stop
making such a fuss

My first steps were taken gingerly onto this hallowed
beach
Where before now, naked women were always out of
my reach
All we had to do was walk round the next sand dune
I tried to decide whether to skulk in, or enter
confidently while whistling a tune

My friend who was here for his own personal reasons
As he has spent a lot of his time with binoculars,
watching this beach through all the seasons
But now he's plucked up the courage to be part of this
lifestyle
He stuttered to a halt and asked, if he could just wait
there a little while

"Come on we're so close" I said, "To a throng of lovely naked birds"
But his courage failed him; all his bravado was nothing more than empty words
Eventually we got ourselves undressed and then paraded off onto the sand
"Where were all the sexy women?" I asked, I didn't understand

There was one old man walking back from a swim
The water must have been cold I thought, just by looking at him
We waited there for most of the day, but no-one else came
My years of lucid dreams were well and truly dashed, what a crying shame.

THE JOURNEY OF A POSTCARD

I sent a postcard from Australia to the U.K
I sent it first class; I thought it would be quicker that
way
Along came someone in a little post van
To empty the post-box, it was of course the post-man

He put it in his van and drove to the sorting office
So far so good, absolutely nothing was a-miss
It got put into a bag bound for the airport
Where a plane would take off, depending on the
weather report

The plane would stop once or twice on its way
Travelling through the night and for most of the day
After a few plane changes the bag landed here
With my postcard safely in it, I had no need to fear

It was loaded again onto another little van
Probably by a cockney, and probably by a man
It would get sorted again at another place
Viewed by the hundredth person as it's a funny card, so
it puts a smile on your face

It would go into a bag for the county of its destination
In the old days it would have then gone straight to the
train station
But instead it gets loaded onto an articulated truck
And gets dropped off at the right sorting office, with a
little bit of luck

The area sorting office puts it in a bag for the town of
the address
Postal companies don't surely deserve all of its bad
press
It gets loaded this time onto a smaller truck
And driven to its final sorting office, and all this for less
than an Ozzie buck

It gets sorted into place by the person who will deliver it
He's just gone out on his round, so it will get there in a
bit
Finally the postcard comes through the letterbox and
lands safely on the floor
But the postman unfortunately, has put it through the
wrong bloody door!

THUNDER AND LIGHTNING

I'm not sure what I find more frightening
Is it the thunder, or is it the lightning?
The lightning is the dangerous bit, but it's over so fast
It's the pretty bit of the show so it's a shame that it
doesn't last
Unless of course you happen to be on the other end of
it
Then I think it may ruin your day, just a little bit

But thunder for me is the most intimidating part
That's the bit for me when the fear begins to start
And yet it can't hurt me in any real way
But when I hear that rumble I just want it to go away
I can feel the change of mood happening in the
atmosphere
I now want be anywhere, anywhere but here

The time between flash and rumble are now closer
together
It won't be long, before I'll be right in the middle of this
scary weather
Help I'm going to die as the lightning is coming my way
I drop to the floor and hurriedly begin to pray
"Let me live and I promise I'll live a good life
P.S. Lord, I've just wet myself, but please don't tell my
wife."

WORST BEST MATE EVER

If I dived in from a ten feet board, then he's dived in
from higher
He's my best friend, but his competitiveness never
seems to tire
Whatever I have done he has done it faster and better
I write a love note, so he wrote his girlfriend a letter

If I drink five beers, then he makes sure he drinks more
If I didn't find it so funny, he would rapidly become a
bore
But he's a really witty guy who never fails to make me
smile
But he's got a new girlfriend, and I haven't seen him in a
while

So I gave him a ring and asked him "What was the
matter?"
He told me his girlfriend was always sick and starting to
get fatter
"Oh dear" I replied, "It sounds like you're going to be a
dad"
I then asked him why this was making him sound, just a
little bit sad

It all happened on the night we went for a beer
He went home drunk with three friends; but they were
all in good cheer

Well I'd told him that my girlfriend had recently slept
with me
So to upstage me once again, he let his girlfriend sleep
with all three!

YOU'VE GOT TO TEN

Just wearing your cowboy boots, lying on my bed
They were the words you wrote, the thoughts I had in
my head
My folks will be downstairs so sneak in through my
window
I'm taking a risk for you, but I'm sure you already know

I followed the note as instructed, right down to the
letter
My imagination running wild, this couldn't be any better
Got naked when I got there, just wearing my boots and
a smile
But she kept me waiting, because I laid there for a while

Then in came her dad holding a shotgun
I simply couldn't move, my legs just went numb
He said "You got my note then, are you disappointed it's
from me
Listen to me now boy; I'm going to make this very easy
I'm going to count very quickly, all the way to ten
Then one way or the other, I'll never see you again

You had better just stay away from my daughter
Because I don't like the things that you've taught her
I can get away with this you know as I'm the local judge
You should also know by now boy, that I also hold a
grudge"

"ONE," I heard him yell, this was serious I could tell
"TWO," my minds gone blank, what am I going to do
"THREE," he said "Take my advice boy, turn around and flee"
"FOUR," I tripped over myself running for the door
"FIVE," will I ever make it, out of here alive
"SIX," if he's joking, it's a sick way to get his kicks
"SEVEN," I'm thinking I can't go naked, up there to heaven
"EIGHT," I made it to the front door, but I'm thinking it's too late
"NINE," he said "You're going to hell boy, and that suits me just fine"
"TEN!" before he pulled that trigger, I tried to pray again

The gun jammed so it didn't work
The relief on my face, I couldn't help but smirk
Then I noticed a warm puddle in my left cowboy boot
But I really didn't care, because I knew he couldn't shoot.

ALMOST THE PERFECT DAY

As the ripples on the pond lapped against my face
It was my first day away, from the relentless rat race
It was a beautiful day with a lovely blue sky
The sun shining brightly, like a luminous yellow dye

What a tranquil place to be and there's no-one around
It's so quiet here that I can't hear a sound
This really is a perfect location
The ideal contrast, from all of my work life frustration

I opened my eyes under the water, just to see what was there
But I didn't see any fish, but to be honest I didn't care
Everything was right about my day, so why was I frowning
Well that's easy to answer, because I'm bloody drowning!

BATTLE OF THE SEXES

I love my wife I'm really sure that I do
Well I'm still married to her, so it really must be true
But increasingly any problems or mistakes all seem to
be my fault
Like when she plugged the hairdryer in with wet hands,
and gave herself a jolt
"You employed the electrician" she ranted and raged at
me
"Wet hands and electricity don't get on" I replied, but
she wouldn't listen to me

She left the freezer door open and everything had
thawed
I was nowhere near her but it's my fault again, good job
my shoulders are broad
Everything's an excuse with her whenever she makes a
mistake
But I never scream and shout at her, I just wish she'd
give *me* a break

She crashed the car the other day and you only had one
guess as to who's to blame
I wasn't even in the car but there was only ever one
mug shot in the frame
I'm battle scarred and weary in a war I just can't win
Women's logic is perfected to beat us every time; they
can even do it with a grin

I'm feeling really tired with all these oral aches and pains
Oh and I've just found out, it's also my fault when it rains!

BLACKPOOL

If you would like a holiday then there's only one place to
go
There's a lot more to Blackpool you know, than just stag
nights and Bingo
Even when the night draws in there are still places to go
You could go to a nightclub or a bar, or go and watch a
show

Morning noon and night, there's always something to
do
That will entertain the kids and adults alike, there's no
time to feel blue
If you have enough time and you can spare the odd
hour
Then you really must visit, the iconic Blackpool Tower

When on the Golden Mile, think about the history and
the people who have all walked there before
And just like you, they probably stopped to gaze at the
sea shore
Off the promenade and onto the very edge of the land
Where you'll find miles upon miles, of beautiful golden
sand

Indulge in an ice cream while standing at the end of a
pier
And you must then send a postcard saying, "We wish
you were here"
The illuminations attract loads of people from hundreds
of miles around
They're better to see when it's been raining, as you can
see their reflections on the ground
The past the present and the future, are all laid out for
all to see
And it can be enjoyed by everyone, you don't need to
be old and smell of wee!

DID WE REALLY GO TO THE MOON

The nineteen sixty's Moon landing space race
Set off at one heck of a pace
It all ended in the year Nineteen Sixty Nine
Where a winner finally raced passed the finishing line

With two astronauts safely on the Moon
There will surely be a space station there sometime
soon
But for some reason or another, no-one else bothered
to go
There must be a reason, surely someone must know?

Then it occurred to me perhaps they never really went
Perhaps it's impossible so no astronauts were really
sent
Could it be that it was all just a hoax
If we read between the lines, we may find a series of
little jokes

Having looked at the evidence I now must conclude
It must have been faked, but I don't want to start a feud
So read what I have to say then make up your own mind
I don't believe it really was, a giant leap for mankind

With the cold war simmering and the Russians winning
the space race
The American organisation called NASA, would need to
somehow try and save face
So I think they lodged an elaborate plan to fool the
whole planet
For good reason though I think, to stop the fighting
between the leaders who ran it

I believe the rocket would need to be at least six feet
thick, to stop a powerful solar flare
There was no need to worry about this though, as the
average person were completely unaware
I think they just orbited the Earth for the days that they
should have been away
Out of sight of everyone just listening to the radio, to
while away the day

They trained and recorded simulations of the trip loads
of times to be sure
So they played mission control a recording, of one
they'd done before
So ground control were unaware thinking the mission
was real
That's because only a couple of people knew, what was
the real deal

While in orbit a released capsule was sent on its way
With the recording of the mission playing merrily away

With equipment to measure the distance between the
Moon and the Earth, it was a fantastic bit of kit
That reflects a laser back to Earth, so that a clever team
can measure it

So why do I think that this is possibly the biggest fake
ever tried
I must make this clear; I would be pleased to think that
they'd lied
In the long run they probably saved millions of lives
And because of it mankind on Earth flourishes and
thrives

Loads of people climb Mount Everest every single year
When I ask why, "Because it can be done" I always hear
Is this why no-one else in the subsequent decades have
ever attempted it
This makes me suspicious, just a little bit
Of course there may be a simpler answer to this taxing
question
That means there is no need for NASA to ever make a
confession
They are very clever people, and people we can trust
So it's just as likely the astronauts suits, really are
coated in lunar dust.

DO YOU WANT TO KNOW?

There are things I know that I feel I must confess
I know if there really is a monster in Loch Ness
I also know the real name of Jack the Ripper
I also know the famous name who used to baby sit him,
when he was a nipper

I have knowledge of whether there is such a thing as a
true UFO
I'm not kidding you its true, I really do know
I can also tell you if things exist that we call the Yeti or
the Sasquatch
And no I'm not a crank or phony, or addicted to the
often blamed bottle of Scotch

I discovered the truth about the Bermuda Triangle
Even though experts have been looking at it, from each
and every angle
Do you want me to tell you the answers to each little
mystery?
It's a shame I'm so shy, or else I could go down in
history

Would you like to know how the Earth really began?
I can also tell you how fast the original Greek Olympians
ran

Alas I'm just too lazy to try a make this into a quiz
So here we go then, the answers to all of the above,
is.........?

GOING BACK HOME

I left my old home town when I was only ten
Now in my thirties, I still think of it now and then
When I pull off the A38 a tingly feeling comes over me
And I start remembering all the fun times, when I was
truly free

My best friend called Andrew lived in my old street
And every time I visit home, he's someone I have to
meet
We always seem to talk about the same old thing each
time
But it never seems boring and everything goes just fine

Then I go for a walk past my old junior school
Where I was never very bright and really considered
quite a fool
My mum blamed the school, but I never got any
brighter
So to compensate in the school yard, I became quite a
fighter

We stay with people I call my Auntie and Uncle, and
they do us a real big favour
Because as well as letting us stay with them, they're
also our old next door neighbour

My childhood girlfriend cried when we moved, as she
simply couldn't understand
Now she's the lead singer in a very successful band

My wife has enjoyed looking into my past, and I've been
talked about like a king
But we must now concentrate more on our future,
that's a much more important thing
Almost the perfect holiday, till my Auntie looked at my
wife and said
"See that bedroom window up there, that's the room in
which he would always wet the bed!"

HEN NIGHT.

In walked a hunky man
He was dressed just like Tarzan
He pressed play on the stereo and he then began
Showing us all, his overall tan

He moved and grooved right on over to me
And he then sat down, on my knee
He teasingly ripped off my L-Plate
He then began, to gyrate

He gave me some oil to rub on him
Anywhere you like, he said with a grin
Tonight I think I'll be home late
Because tonight, is going to be great

Who's on their hen night, you are!
Who's going to drink dry, this bar!
Who's on their hen night, you are!
Who's going to be the drunkest, by far?
Well it's obvious, you are!

The stripper's now gone, so I think it's time to move on
To those party games, I know you know which ones
But first please let me give you some advice
Which I hope will carry you through all your married life
Make sure that you're faithful to him

And make sure you stay away from that extra marital
sin

Make sure you've picked the right bloke?
Because getting married really is no joke
But as long as you both simply honour and obey
Then I know your marriage, will be okay
But that's all for another night
Because tonight's all about the end of your single life.

HOW TO LIVE YOUR LIFE

I've learned one very important lesson in my time on
this Earth
And that is that you have to be happy, and appreciate
your own worth
Happiness isn't all about power and money
But embracing nature, and no I'm not trying to be funny

We all should be judged by the way we treat each other
Treat men like your brother, and women like your
mother
A kind word to lift someone's spirit will go a long way
And if you're that way inclined, each night kneel down
and pray

The one single thing that can be done that surpasses all
other
Is if you can't think of a nice word to say, then stop, and
think of another
Because one bad word gets returned with another, then
another and so on
Until it escalates into a bitter feud and suddenly your
friendship is gone

Some more good advice is never judge by what you see
I'm living proof of this because it happened to me

A flat tyre, stuck on the side of the road with cars
whizzing by
Then stopped this tattooed long haired menacing
looking guy
Simply to see if I needed a hand and he was as nice as
anyone could be
And yet when I saw him pull over and stop, all I wanted
to do was flee

Do good things for other people and good things will
happen to you
What a great way to live your life, even if it turns out
not to be true.

I WAS A POSTMAN

A few years ago I used to work as a post-man
In winter I'd get wet, and in summer I'd get a tan
Customers would always introduce me to their beloved
dog
I'd do things in my pants, which you would usually do on
the bog
He won't hurt you they always say; he's really just a big
softy
Next thing I know, he's sitting right on me

The most boring phrase I hear is, "If it's a bill you can
keep it"
I smile politely and then laugh out of habit
I used to deliver a thousand letters a day
If I make just one mistake, I'd always hear them say
"You always get it wrong and it's not just today"
As much as you want to scream and shout
And even give some of them a right good clout
I have to say "Sorry about that, but have a nice day"
Then as calmly as I can, just walk away

The summer of 2007, and along came the strikes
Many customers hypothetically got on their bikes
The company lost a load of money and respect
Employees were getting restless, which the bosses
could detect

The walk was good exercise, but what I hated the most
Was the fact I had to carry a bag full of post!

IT'S A CAT'S LIFE

Imagine if you will a fat sleepy cat
Lying on a soft padded pillow, how about that
The pillow is in front of a roaring log fire
And a quiet soothing song on the radio, is being sung by
a choir

The rain is drumming hard onto the window
And the shutters rattle, as the wind begins to blow
But the cat is dry and warm and has a full fat belly
To make this evening perfect, he needs something good
on the telly

The cat gets a loving stroke from his owner as he walks
by
The cat loves the attention, as it gives him a natural high
Picture a litter tray by the back door so he doesn't even
have to go out
So there are no accidents that the cat's owner needs to
shout about

The cat without realising it, gives out a satisfied purr
When his owner very gently, brushes his soft fur
I often think I am that cat in this wonderful vision
As I can feel every detail with absolute precision

But can you just image this idyllic scene?
It's not reality though, it *is* just a dream

If I was *really* that cat, then I would be curled up hungry in a drafty hall
Choking to death on my own fur ball!

JACK THE RIPPERS OCCOMPLICE

My eyes flickered from left to right as I beckoned the
Ripper in
After he had just committed, yet another hideous evil
sin
He got into the back with me of my horse drawn cab
The transport that brought death again, to the mortuary
slab

His eyes were dancing with excitement, complimented
by the look on his face
He then ordered me to take him, straight back home to
his place
Preaching "They'll soon all be gone from this great city
of mine,
Then everything will be civilised, and everything will be
fine"

The poor unfortunate women were only working for
money to buy food
But they had to do things that were sordid, lewd and
very crude
Their spirits though were of no less value than any other
human being
The Ripper though thought that they were worthless,
and were in desperate need of killing

My role in all this was to make sure that he didn't get caught
That is only because I fear; I'm a woman who's easily bought
He thought that women like girls, should be seen and not heard
And in a class race behind men and boys, women would come third

Prostitutes always exuded complete confidence and power
He didn't like the fact that in his presence, they would never tremble or cower
He told me that prostitutes and whores are lowering this great city's tone
I never responded but thought, No Jack, you're doing that on your own

The Ripper wore a costume, a hat, a cape, and trousers, which he was careful not to crease
But he wore it with trepidation, as it's a crime to impersonate the Police
This was how he could wonder the streets completely at will
And he then picked out an unfortunate victim, which he would then follow and kill

He never for one moment thought that he would ever go to hell
On his deathbed he thought he was going to heaven, as he whispered me farewell
I know for a fact that when I die, I will also go straight to hell
At least I'll be back with my husband, so all's well that ends well.

ME, MY WIFE AND MORTALITY

I hate my wife when we have a verbal brawl
Because I don't have the luxury of total recall
I can never remember any facts or dates
Or the times when she went out, with all of *her* mates
But she can rattle off all the times I got things wrong
I know the times when I'm wrong, because I'm
reminded of them all year long

She can twist the facts so that it's always my entire fault
No jury needed, I'm guilty by default
She tells me I'm no good at this and no good at that
But she really gets feisty when I call her a spoilt brat

She throws things at me when she's losing the battle
That's when I have to protect my precious wedding
tackle
I'm not talking about throwing cushions or the local
paper
I mean things that really are a potential widow maker

Cups, bowls and even the odd knife
To think I was so proud to call this thing my wife
It's not worth winning the row, as I'd have to sleep in
the spare room
It's then like living with a wicked witch, after someone
has snapped her broom!

MY OLD NEIGHBOUR AND ME

My old neighbour used to spy on me like a hawk
And whenever I went into my garden, he would have to
come out and talk
He would lean on our fence and take in everything I
have in the garage
And he wouldn't leave me alone; it was like an
obsessive horrific marriage

Any spare piece of wood or plastic he would want to
borrow
He would always say "I promise, I'll return it to you
tomorrow"
How can you return something that you're going to use?
Time after time in this situation I always seemed to lose

He'd then say something like, "I saw in garage the other
day"
So far I haven't, but I would really like to say, "What's it
to you then by the way?"
The problem is our low fence dividing our land
I must from somewhere get the courage up to be
counted and make a stand

I think at least I should need a six foot fence
He's got too much not to borrow though for that to
make sense

I must let him know by being firm the next time he talks
to me
Better still my little boy can tell him, because he won't
cave in so easily!

SNOOKER

Pot a red then a colour, and again another red
It's a skilful game; it really has to be said
Caressing the baize with your cue resting hand
A gentleman's sport that's really grand

The atmosphere is always calm and relaxed
But it's a game that can leave you feeling tired and
mentally taxed
Nobody cheats because that wouldn't be fair
A gentleman's game remember, so cheating is rare

A 147 maximum is the aim of the game
But if you don't get one, you certainly shouldn't feel any
shame
When you get more points than your opponent in any
single game
You have then won what snooker players have always
called a frame

You must stand properly and keep the snooker cue
straight
The feeling you get when you pot a ball, is really truly
great
There's only thing in snooker which really baffles me
Is that the older you get, the worse you seem to be

It's not a physically demanding sport; you don't need to be super fit to succeed in
But like the other sports, why is it that the youngest always seem to win
If you're good, then you could easily earn some really healthy wages
And if you're the best, then you'll go down in Snooker's history pages.

STEVE IRWIN

I'll never forget the day that Steve Irwin died
Although I am a man, I stood motionless and cried
Why had such a good man been so tragically taken?
My belief in God and justice, has been badly shaken

He adored his children in his life
And the bond so strong that he shared with his wife
He taught me things I wanted to know
All through the magic of his television show

There wasn't any hate or negativity in his soul
Changing people's opinion on animals, was his number
one goal
And in this pursuit I know he succeeded
He was the animal's friend they so badly needed

His drive for conservation really caused a sensation
This got him the support from people, from almost
every nation
His love for life was just pure gold
It's a tragedy that he'll never grow old

His memory lives on though through me and you
His peace loving message will always shine through
I'll never forget him that much is true
And one day I hope to go and visit, Australia Zoo.

WHATS THE POINT OF WAR?

As I walk through the pearly gates
To be reunited, with all of my fallen mates
Please don't think that I'd died in vain
My life has hopefully saved more people from pain

Why must we fight at all in the first place?
There are no real winners in this type of race
The country that loses and have to give in
Needs to be repaired, by the winners from ruin

What's the point? We all ask with a sigh
"Over the top" the sergeant would cry
Into the killing fields for some the last time
After I died I didn't have to do it anymore, which suited
me fine

Let's all do something strange and live in harmony
And not fight over something trivial, like the desire for
money
Because money really doesn't matter a thing
If in the process we lose everything

Why should my son grow up with no dad?
And my wife cry over me, whenever she feels sad
All because heads of state can't get along
They don't fight or get hurt, it's just plain wrong

So politicians listen to this if you dare
Forget your image for a second and become humanely aware
We don't want someone who's nothing but a warmonger
Filling up your war chest, even while *your* people are dying from hunger.

BIRTHDAY MONEY

While out and about with my little boy
I took him shopping, so that he can pick out a new toy
All day long we went from toy shop to toy shop
He was still full of energy, but I was fit to drop

We took a break in a cafe to have a bite to eat
I let him choose the place, as today was his treat
Re-fuelled and ready to go, we then carried on our day out
But every toy shop was busy; it seems every child was out and about

The last toy shop and my little boy still could not decide
"Don't worry dad" he said, "We can come back tomorrow and have another bus ride"
"Were not coming into town again" I said," We can get your toy off the internet"
This wasn't the day that I had planned, but that last statement sounded like a threat

So we went off again to get something else to eat
I don't know how he can keep going; I'm dead on my feet
We can try the last place down there on the high street
He finally saw a toy that made him say "Wow, that's neat"

My little boy's eyes truly lit up when he saw this perfect toy
But this was a toy for a girl, not the toy for a boy
I gently told him that this wasn't a toy for "A him"; it's intended for "A her"
He told me as he couldn't find a toy for him; so he'd spend his birthday money, on his sister.

SPRING CLEAN

I'm in the middle of doing my annual spring clean
It's only the middle of January, but I think you know
what I mean
Everything I threw out she would say she wants to keep
I must remember next year to do this when she's asleep

It would always end up with me saying, "Oh keep it if
you must
But it's just going to sit there again gathering more
dust"
"Oh no it won't" would come the reply
"Whatever" would be my surrendering cry

We only live in a little old house
It's not even big enough to own our own mouse
But she keeps on buying loads of new stuff
The space in our house, there just isn't enough

Doesn't matter what I say she just refuses to listen
Each time I move something, she spy's that it's missin'
It's simply a battle that I can't really win
She's learnt that when something has gone missing, to
first go and check the bin!

U.F.O.

A bright light sped across the evening sky
So fast, it then suddenly stopped; I'm not telling a lie
It then shot straight up all the way into space
I knew for sure this was something which nothing on
Earth could beat in a race

It returned to Earth and started dancing around
It came close but it didn't once hit the ground
The craft stopped and hovered directly above me
A shaft of light then lifted me upwards, very easily

I was then put on a table and poked and prodded
The aliens never talked to each other, they simply
looked and nodded
Next thing I know I'm back on Earth just laying on the
floor
I've been abducted I think, no I was I'm absolutely sure

I told my wife and she just laughed at me
My friends that I told honestly thought that I'd gone
crazy
There are no marks or scars or even a calling card
So for someone to believe me I admit will be hard

I never had much choice, but this was my one night I
was brave
But I'll sadly have to take this experience, all the way to
my grave
I hadn't had a drink and I never even got a fright
But I'm the only one who really knows, what happened
on that night.

D.I.Y

All I had to do was fix a cupboard to the wall
I needed to use a stool because I'm not very tall
With one screw in, it was going uncharacteristically well
Holding the other end up with my arm, I gave my wife a
yell

"Can you get me a Philips screwdriver please my little
sweet pea?"
My wife's not that bright, but she was the only one
around to help me
At the bottom of the stairs "A Philips screwdriver you
said?"
"Yes, hurry up" I replied, she walked away confused
scratching her head

This cupboard was getting heavy and my arms were
starting to tire
My arms were now metaphorically, feeling like they're
on fire
What an earth could be taking her so long
It's a simple task, what could possibly go wrong

She wandered back with absolutely nothing in her grip
Never ask your wife for help, that's a pretty good tip

"I can't find any Philips screwdrivers in your tool shed I can only find Stanley ones" was the daft statement she said!

HOLIDAYING LIFESTYLE

I want to get myself into a holidaying lifestyle
I must choose really carefully though, as I'll be doing it
for a while
Do I go for a Caravan, Motor home or a Canal boat?
There are lots of things to consider, so I'd better take
note

The least expensive thing I think would be the Caravan
But out there on the open road I would be a much
hated man
The most expensive thing I think would be the Motor
home
And as cost equals size, I think I would have to holiday
alone

This leaves the only other option, and that's a Canal
boat
But the only thing I know about watercraft, is that
they're supposed to float
All this thinking and planning is becoming to be a pain
So I think I'll just have another cheap holiday, on a
beach somewhere in Spain.

HONESTY

I met this beautiful woman called Terry with an I
After we got real friendly it turned out it was Terry with
a Y
I bought a lotion to stop me from losing my hair
No side effects it said, not that the company were
aware
Well I broke out all over in a horrible gooey rash
To think that lotion cost me an awful lot of cash

Why must we all con each other all the time?
If we didn't then we could all live happily after just fine
I'd like to believe everything I read
But it's always written by someone's obsessive need for
greed

Half price this and money off that, and get big discounts
here
It's still over priced, even a simple cold beer
I'd like to be able to walk down the street
And then say "Hello" to everyone that I meet
But people just aren't polite anymore
They look the other way or make replying a chore

Well I've made it my mission, to say "Hi" to people I see
So don't be rude or violent, just be polite back to me

Then let's try to stop conning one another
Treat everyone as if they are your long lost brother

Before you go ahead and rape pillage and steal
Please take a moment, to think how the victim will feel
The world is beautiful and full of great things to see
Let's not spoil it please; it really is up to you and me.

UNCLE RAY AND AUNTIE JAN

I would like to tell you about my Uncle Ray and Auntie
Jan
He is a rough tough, no-nonsense but intelligent man
You can talk to him about virtually anything
And you're guaranteed the he will know about the
topic, or at least something

Auntie Jan is happy and friendly, and nothing is ever any
trouble at all
Though she is a grandma, she hasn't got the slippers or
the shawl
If you needed it and she had it, she would gladly give it
to you
And if you need advice or guidance, she will be there to
help you through

They're not my real Auntie and Uncle, that much is a lie
But if you will give me the chance I'll explain, or at least
I'll try
They were my neighbours, from when I was one year
old till ten
Then they moved away, but we still see them now and
then

Growing up I was taught, that calling a grown up by
their first name was wrong
But they are as close as my real family, our bond really
is that strong
So calling them Mr and Mrs, to me didn't seem quite
right
So Uncle and Auntie I was to call them, just to be polite

I'm now fully grown but I still call them the same
It just wouldn't be right, to call them by their first name
By doing so keeps their family status and I hope they
never defect
Because the way they are have earned, my complete
and total respect.

CAN'T REMEMBER

I have a problem, err…..erm……remembering things
I've only been married once, but I've lost countless
wedding rings
I'm always forgetting things, like where I've parked the
car
And forgetting to go and visit, my old ma and pa

Every time I set out to erm, diagnose what I've..err..got
I get to where I need to go, but go home again because I
forgot
I left my wife when we were err….erm…..err…. on
holiday
Hours later I remembered, went and found her but I
didn't know what to say

I really must at all costs do my best to resist
To purposely forget things, like going to the dentist
My wife would say, "Put the oven on at four o'clock"
I'd write it down, and when I actually do it, it gives her
quite a shock

I'm always late going here or I don't turn up there
People must think I'm rude, or that I just don't really
care
Last night I thought of a very funny line to end this
poem on
So here it is, its err…..erm….err, no sorry, it's gone.

MY WORST POEM EVER

Three and four, this is the worst poem I've written for
sure
Did you see what I did to make it rhyme?
I'll do it again, but do it better this time
Nine and ten, my little blue pen, there you go, shall I do
it again?

It doesn't always have to make sense
I'll claim its abstract and keep up the pretence
A poem is like a song you see; it must always rhyme to
be any good to me
Twenty one and twenty two, at least this poem isn't
blue
Twenty two and twenty three, will somebody please
make me a cup of tea
Two lines there that don't even match
This will leave a real poet with his head to scratch

Why doesn't this poem mean anything?
Why did the first telephones make the sound, "Ring
ring?"
Seven and eight, I'm going to bed now as it's getting late

Life is all about the familiar; it might not be right or
wrong
But it gives everything else perspective of where we
belong
If we were used to nothing making sense
This poem might mean something, it may even cause
offence.

WHY DO WE HUMANS ALWAYS RUIN EVERYTHING?

Why does progress always seem to devalue our quality
of life?
Pollution, expense, disease, in the twenty first century,
these are all still rife
Everyone seems to love the old days of the railroad
track
Where steam locomotives were king, most want to
bring them back

Instead we have soulless diesel machines zipping along
the rails
But even to this day, the slightest bit of bad weather
and the service simply fails
The romantic era of the motor car, dawned a few years
ago
But now it's headlights to bumpers for most places that
you go

The sheer joy of driving has now left us forever
Speed cameras coupled with road rage, when you see
some idiot trying to be clever
The dream of one day, which we all could take to flight
We soon like everything else, over did this all right

Air pollution has gone worse, certainly not better
Seems strange to say it but these days, even the rain
seems wetter

Why as humans do we have to take everything too far?
From old wooden sailing boats, all the way to the motor
car.

JUST A LITTLE CHUBBY

I love my kids but they sometimes offend me
By telling me that I'm just a little bit chubby
When they play tents they use one of my shirts
They say it gives them more room, I admit that it hurts

They ask if I want to go for a waddle instead of a walk
And they all stare at my three chins each time that I talk
When I lay in the bath they think my belly is an island
I also get the whale jokes on the beach, as I try to get
tanned

The slimmest clothes I can look at is extra extra large
My buddies and I went jet skiing once, they all joked
that I should use a barge
My wife tells me that I'm cuddly and kind
I'd trade it all in though, so that I could sit down without
wedging my behind

I have to pay for two seats when I fly by aeroplane
Then catch a person looking down at me, which is when
I really feel the most shame
I'm the first to admit that I do overeat
And that when I exercise, I do actually cheat

I'm just not designed to be an athletic machine
I shower a lot because I sweat and I want to be clean
I sometimes wish people could only see
Just how much pain that their looks and jokes, do
actually affect me?

WEDDING WISHES

As your bride is making herself all pretty and cute
You'll be somewhere else, donning your whistle and
flute
Your love for each other is as pure as a virgin white dove
You're about to get your marriage blessed by God up
above

You'll laugh, have fun, and you may even cry
But marriage is a journey worth taking; I wouldn't tell
you a lie
Like us all, you will no doubt encounter some stormy
weather
The best way to survive it, is to make sure you stay
together

If there's only one piece of advice that I can give you
Is to cherish each moment in your marriage, as you will
certainly collect a few
May your marriage to each other be forever strong
And as far as duration goes, I hope it will be long

So today is the start of a journey, you take in your new
life
One in which you take with your beautiful wife
So good luck, God bless, we are all wishing you well
This poem comes straight from my heart, I hope you can
tell.

A DAY'S SAILING

It took at least half an hour to put it all together
So it was just as well that it was beautiful sunny weather
But once we'd set off the wind just died
He told me it was all under control, but it was just to
save his pride

It wasn't that long before the boat began to leak
Dismayed he just stared; he simply couldn't speak
Gathering his thoughts he said that everything's just
fine
But somehow you know, I don't believe him this time

I'm just so happy though that we're still afloat
Bobbing up and down in his little blue boat
The wind would come, but then the wind would go
But it didn't really matter, as we only ever went slow

In my own words though, we're not exactly sailing
To be brutally honest, all I'm doing is bailing
I suddenly noticed that the daylight was dimming
As I thought to myself, that we'll soon be swimming

We did make it in time back to the shore
To then have to pack it all up, oh what a chore
It took us ages to trailer the boat and put everything
away
About flipping time, as were now at the end of the day

But we had a nice time though I can honestly say
As we sailed and we kayaked for most of the day
Time to drive home now as it's a long journey ahead
And I'm now starting to dream, of climbing into bed.

The End.